State Book Purcha

TEXAS STATE LIBRARY PURCHA

M000189243

W. RAY SCOTT, NATIONAL PARK CONCESSIONS, INC.

THE WAY I HEARD IT

Walter Fulcher, about 1940. (Photograph by Denison Studio, Dallas)

Texas - Tales
Big Bend - Tales
Folklore — Texas

398.23
F4h

THE WAY I HEARD IT

Tales of the Big Bend

By WALTER FULCHER

*Edited with Introduction and Notes
by Elton Miles*

RHOADS MEMORIAL LIBRARY
14726

UNIVERSITY OF TEXAS PRESS, AUSTIN

International Standard Book Number 0-292-79001-5
Library of Congress Catalog Card Number 73-8324
Copyright © 1959, 1973 by the University of Texas Press
All Rights Reserved

Second Edition

Printed in the United States of America

Dedicated to the memory of

CORA ETTA FULCHER

*West Texas pioneer woman and
mother of the author*

Contents

List of Illustrations

Who Was Walter Fulcher?

Walter Fulcher was a living example of the reason given by Big Bend people for the scarcity of traffic on their highways: Everybody is already where he wants to be.

Though Fulcher may have been what he called "a poor boy trying to raise a few cows on a desert," he lived in a silver mine of tales, place names, and fabulous personalities. Who wants to move away from even a desert when it has such landmarks as Butcher Knife Spring, Dead Horse Canyon, and Cow Heaven Pasture? What better life for Walter Fulcher than wrangling cows in a painted desert and tapering off under an evening's lamp with a book of Blasco Ibáñez or Omar's *Rubaiyat*? Walter Fulcher grew so full of Big Bend lore that he had to make a book himself. To him a tale is no good unless it is told.

Born in Lampasas County, Texas, on December 21, 1887, Arl Walter Fulcher was about fourteen when his family moved him to Sterling County in 1901. His father, Frank Porter Fulcher, was a native Texan; and his mother, Cora Etta Fulcher, was brought from Missouri to Texas at the age of five. In Sterling County his father is remembered as one of the pioneer ranchmen of West Texas.

At the age of twenty-five, early in 1912, Walter worked near Sheffield, Texas, on the Martin Ranch, which figures in his chapter on "Outlaws and *Bandidos*." There he witnessed some of the events in the last outrage of the Black Jack Ketchum gang, told for the first time in this book.

By his twenty-sixth birthday, he was working for the Baker and White Ranch, also near Sheffield. Though Fulcher had but eight years of formal schooling, he loved to read, and he developed the knack of writing vividly and to the point. In a letter from this ranch to his family at Sterling City in 1913, he told of a recent trip to Fort Worth and of how he and his companion stayed in a fine hotel. Of the return trip, he wrote:

Coming back, we were in Angelo from three o'clock in the morning until seven, so we strolled over to the Landon. While we were sitting there, Jeff said with a gesture of disdain that would have done credit to a Duke, "These country hotels are awful bum when a person is accustomed to the city. They have no style at all."

"Yes," I said, "and it is so fatiguing to climb the stairs." Just as though we hadn't been used to eating out of tin plates on our laps, sleeping with nothing but a soogan and a piece of eighteen-ounce ducking between us and the fury of the elements, and climbing mountains a mile high, carrying cedar posts, et cetera.

He had been back home two days, but, he said:

I can't bring myself to go out in the sheep camp. It is too much of a sudden drop, from scenes of gay festivity and lively companions to sheep and sullen and sad-faced greaser herders. I believe that sheeping is absolutely the most joyless existence in the world.

From his sheeping days, however, Walter gained one of his most fortunate assets, his knowledge of Spanish. His sister, Mrs. Elvie Williams, writes:

Walter learned this language in the Black Gap country, near Sheffield, in 1911. He was the only American within miles of this sheep camp, and with the aid of an old Mexican man, a Spanish dictionary, and a Spanish reader, he mastered the language in six months. He later read all the Spanish novels and classics that came his way.

As to his proficiency not only in reading but in speaking the language, his sister says, "Mexicans often have said that they have talked to him in the darkness of night without being aware that they were talking to a *gringo*." Consequently there are several Spanish expressions in his book which are by no means correct in the school-book sense. They are true, however, to the local dialect spoken in the Big Bend region of the Río Grande.

When the United States entered the First World War, Fulcher joined the army at Fort Stockton, Texas, on May 31, 1918. Trained at Camp Lee, Virginia, he attained the rank of sergeant with the Army Mobile Veterinary Hospital, Section I. With this unit he became acting First Sergeant in supervision of a hundred and fifty men. In a letter to his mother, he remarked, "There are several drawbacks to a first sergeant's job. The officers kick on one side and the men on the other."

While awaiting orders to proceed to the port of embarkation, Fulcher received a package from home. He wrote, "I got the jam a few days before I left Camp Lee. The Secretary of War was not in hollering distance, so another sergeant, a cook, and four privates helped me eat it—and a soldier on guard from another outfit, where we had our picnic, licked the jar."

Before embarking, men in Fulcher's unit put on a rodeo in Petersburg, Virginia, on July 4, 1918. Fulcher's big Texas hat performed in the bronc-busting, but not the First Sergeant himself, as he was tied down in camp by duty.

While crossing the Atlantic to France in August, soldier Fulcher had home in his mind. He wrote, "I never before realized the immensity of the ocean as I do now, and only wish that the water of the earth's surface were more equally divided. For instance, a few more dry spots in the Atlantic and a few more wet ones in western Texas."

In France, Fulcher served until May 11, 1919, with his veterinary unit. Back in the States, while awaiting transportation to Fort Sam Houston for discharge, he wrote from his temporary station on the east coast: "I've got the blues, the blues, the Alpine blues, and the West-bound on my mind!" He was heading now not for Sterling County nor for Sheffield, but to his new home in the Big Bend.

In 1919 Fulcher's parents had moved to Terlingua in Brewster County, where they acquired a ranch. They drove the cattle and horses through the country and moved their household goods in wagons. Joining his parents in the Big Bend, Walter Fulcher became one of the last ranchmen to use the free range. In a short time, as settlers bought up the state land, Walter also acquired a section here and there. At its largest, the Fulcher Ranch extended from Hen Egg Mountain on the north, following Terlingua Creek, down to the Big Bend National Park line on the south. Near the ranch headquarters are the old rock corrals, once a part of the G–4 Ranch referred to in Fulcher's chapter on "Will James: Big Bend Superman."

During the brief depression that followed the war, the Fulchers succeeded in holding their own in the Big Bend country. With the help of his father, Walter stayed in the ranching business, built up his herd, and bought more land. To supplement his income, he worked at El Paso as a carpenter in the Bridge and Building Department of the Southern Pacific Railroad from May, 1923, to August, 1926. But from 1919 onward, Walter Fulcher's permanent and spiritual home was his dry ranch on the Terlingua desert.

When he came there, Terlingua was a flourishing mining town. The quicksilver boom was at its height and the rain was adequate for a time, so that both mines and ranches prospered. In time, both dried up, and life became a series of struggles against recurrent drouth.

In 1928 Fulcher was elected trustee of Terlingua School District, in which position he served for the twenty-five remaining years of his life. In this service, he saw to the hiring of teachers and the securing of houses for the teachers, to obtaining a piano, buying books, and repairing and rebuilding the schoolhouse.

In 1941, with the entrance of the United States into the Second World War, Fulcher helped to organize Company C, 3rd Battalion, of the Texas Defense Guard, permanently stationed at Terlingua. On November 21, 1941, he was permanently commissioned and on March 30, 1943, was promoted to captain. His unit was made up of men from all over the Big Bend region, and its mission was indoctrination and basic training. The unit was made up always of about ninety per cent Latin Americans, not one of whom slipped across the Río Grande to elude army service.

During the last few years of his life, Walter Fulcher began to write down tales of the Big Bend. In this work, he was encouraged by his friend Glenn Burgess, of Alpine. He wrote the stories carefully and legibly on letter-tablet paper and then had them typed. The result was a typescript upon which this book is based, bearing the same title. Save for rearrangement of some sections, Fulcher's text is practically untouched. To disturb Fulcher's basic style would be to pinch off a spontaneous western manner of expression that is full of vigor and humor.

In this book, Walter Fulcher presents some historical material and folklore never before brought into print. For the first time, there is printed an account of the Domínguez gang. Here are presented new eye-witness details of the last episode in the history of Black Jack Ketchum's gang, as seen by Walter himself.

New folk characters are introduced: El Piocho and El Cíbolo the Indian traders, and Will James, the Big Bend maverick-hunter. Also he presents new information on many Big Bend place names.

In 1951, when his manuscript was completed, Fulcher found himself in ill health. After spending some time in the Veterans' Hospital at Big Spring, he visited his brother, Aubrey Fulcher, in Midland, and died there on August 27, 1953. He was buried in Alpine.

On a blustery March day less than twelve months after Walter Fulcher's death, a line of automobiles traveled through the mountains from Alpine to the ghost town of Terlingua. A detachment from the American Legion post of Alpine conducted a ceremony to perpetuate their regard of Walter Fulcher's place in the slow and intermittent progress of the Big Bend desert villages. Tumbleweeds scampered before the blowing dust. School Superintendent Peyton Cain made a speech, and while the nine pupils of Terlingua School looked on, Walter's little niece, Emery Fulcher, unveiled a bronze plaque mounted on a low stone. The plaque reads:

WALTER FULCHER

1887–1953

PIONEER–SOLDIER–EDUCATOR

In memory of his lifetime of

service to his school

and community

From Terlingua School Children

1953

ELTON MILES

Sul Ross State College
Alpine, Texas

A Note of Acknowledgment

For their assistance, I should like to express my indebtedness and appreciation to the following: Mrs. Elvie Williams of Alpine, Texas, and her brother, Mr. Stanley Fulcher of Terlingua, Texas, who made this book possible; Mr. David Jones, Santa Fe, New Mexico; Mr. and Mrs. Arthur Blucher, Phoenix, Arizona; Mr. Dudley Dobie of San Marcos, Texas; Mr. Wally George of Odessa, Texas; Mrs. Jeannine Cox Caraway of Iraan, Texas; Mrs. F. G. Walker and Mr. Worth Frazer of Alpine; Dean Bevington Reed and Professors Clifford B. Casey, Ernest C. Shearer, Stather Elliott Thomas, and Charles King, all of Sul Ross State College; Mr. Larence Hardin of Crane, Texas, and Miss Annetta Lee of Houston, both Sul Ross students; and especially to my wife, Lillian.

E. M.

Publisher's Note

This edition of *The Way I Heard It* is identical in every respect with the first edition published in 1959 except for the fact that most of the illustrations have been changed. All the new pictures are from the collection of Ross Maxwell, Austin. That of Trapper McMahon comes from the Smithers Collection in The University of Texas Humanities Research Center. The frontispiece portrait of Walter Fulcher was made available by Mrs. Daisy Fulcher Adams, Terlingua, Texas.

Foreword

I believe there are various localities in the United States called "Big Bend," but the one I propose to write about is really Big. That is the region lying within the big bend of the Río Grande in West Texas.

Without definite or fixed boundaries, it is usually defined something like this: Using the Southern Pacific Railroad to mark its northern boundary, start in somewhere near Fort Hancock, Texas, where the Río Grande starts its mighty loop to the southward. Follow Ol' Man River as he cuts tremendous gorges and chews up whole mountains, until, after circling the Chisos Mountains and the present site of the Big Bend National Park, where he cuts some of his more spectacular didoes, he turns in a northerly direction, approaching the Southern Pacific Railroad at Langtry, Texas. The region between the railroad and the bend of the river is known as the Big Bend country.

It comprises the major part of some of the largest counties in Texas. Parts of Hudspeth, Culberson, Jeff Davis, Presidio, Brewster, and Terrell counties lie within its borders. Either of these counties could hide completely a state like Delaware or Rhode Island within its boundaries. Brewster County alone, nine-tenths of which lies in the Big Bend, is larger than the state of New Jersey (so I am told, I never measured either).[1]

You can gather from this that the Big Bend is a considerable stretch of country, though "stretch" is hardly the word. It is wrinkled, folded, and twisted into ridges, hogbacks, and peaks and into ranges and isolated clumps of mountains. Its climate ranges from Paisano Pass between Alpine and Marfa, where thirty inches of snow has fallen in a day, to San Vicente and Boquillas, where ice is seldom seen. It was in the path of the first white man to cross the North American continent, hardly more than a generation after Columbus' first voyage. It was the stronghold of the last hostile Indians in the United States within the memory of men and women still living.

It can readily be seen that in the four hundred years or so, there are tremendous and interesting possibilities for history and legends, all of them—including the ones I am about to relate—open to criticism and doubt.

[1] The states smaller than Brewster County are Connecticut, Delaware, and Rhode Island. Brewster County is larger than Connecticut and Rhode Island combined.

The following stories, except for those events I partly observed myself, are folk tales pure and simple, related orally and written largely from memory. Not one single hour has been spent in research to secure documentary evidence for or against their accuracy, though I have accidentally stumbled on written accounts that seem to partly confirm some of them.

But because it is not documented history, need it be rejected in its entirety? Before any account was written, it had to be told orally in most cases. Even eyewitness accounts have in many cases been proved erroneous, and after reading the mistakes, distortions and downright lies about this region by writers of my own day, I have become very skeptical about those old records. If they were no more accurate than some modern ones, the Lord help us.

Some old geezer, I've forgotten who, once said, "History is a mass of lies agreed upon." A noted American, Henry Ford, said flatly that "History is bunk," and centuries ago a certain old philosopher-poet versified like this:

> The revelations of devout and learned,
> Who rose before us and as prophets burned,
>   Are all but stories, which, awoke from sleep
> They told their fellows and to sleep returned.

Pretty extreme statements all. I don't fully endorse any of them, but at least I have some rather distinguished company in thinking that history is sometimes very, very cockeyed. You have only to read the accounts of different nations of their wars with each other to see that something is rotten not necessarily just in Denmark.

I would like to give credit to all the sources of these stories, but in some cases I don't remember their names. In others, the stories are built up of fragments from many casual remarks. The story of the treasure cave in the Chisos Mountains, for instance, is made up of brief accounts from many different sources.

In conclusion, I believe firmly that the characters mentioned in these stories really existed and the events narrated actually occurred. Of course, the details may be badly garbled by time and many repetitions. Be that as it may, I shall tell it the way I heard it.

WALTER FULCHER

Terlingua, Texas
1953

THE WAY I HEARD IT

1. Oxcarts and Chihuahua Wagons

The Double Wedding at Old Terlingua

This story was told by an old Mexican peddler, who said his grandfather had told it to him. I found it interesting because if it was true, it indicated that even in that remote day there were Spanish-speaking settlers at the mouth of Terlingua Creek and the place was called Terlingua. It must have happened about 1800, since the old man said he was born about 1830 and that this happened when his grandfather was a young man.

I do not remember this old peddler's name. Like most everybody else, I called him *Tío*, which means

"uncle." He was a grouchy and taciturn old cuss,
whose enterprises were mostly illegal and whose
morals or scruples were not apparent to the unaided
eye. But for some reason he took a liking to me, and
while Mexican shearing crews or labor gangs were en-
joying his illegal cargoes, he would sit around and tell
me of the days when he was a teamster in the Indian
countries, or tales his father or grandfather, who had
both been teamsters, had told him.

He did not tell this straight ahead like a story as I
tell it, but in scattered and sketchy fragments, almost
bare of details, and I have been obliged to arrange the
events in sequence and reconstruct the story as well as
I can from memory, so that while the story is his, the
words are mine.

It begins with a train of ox-drawn *carretas* stopping
at the mouth of Terlingua Creek, where there was a
small village of Mexicans and, it would seem, Indians
and mixed breeds. These *carretas* were huge two-
wheeled carts, made almost entirely of wood and rawhide and pulled by from two to eight oxen. It looks like
they were trading wagons out of Chihuahua, backed by
Chihuahua merchants, following the Indian trails to
trade with the people in border towns like San Carlos,
Santa Helena, and San Vicente in Mexico and Terlingua in Texas. The owner and *capitán* of this train
was called *"El Piocho"* (*piocho* meaning "chin

whisker"). Besides him, there were six or eight ox-drivers, among them the grandfather of old Tío.

There were among these teamsters two young boys just off the farm, and while they were camped here these boys spent all their spare time helping the natives gather their crops of corn and *calabazas,* or pumpkins. There was among the settlers an old man who very late in life had married a native woman and settled in Ter-lingua. In answer to my question, old Tío said he did not know whether she was Mexican or Indian. His grandfather only said she was *una mujer de allí,* a woman of there or that place. At any rate, they had two daughters about fifteen and sixteen years old who did most of the farm work, since the father was very old and probably not very good about working anyhow.

Soon the two young teamsters were helping only the young farmerettes, and the result was that they decided to get married. El Piocho was generous and gave the young people a swell *boda,* or wedding feast, at which he danced with both brides and got so drunk that when the two or three day feast was over, he continued his spree for several weeks more.

When he finally sobered up, he found that in the meantime it had rained somewhere on the upper reaches of the Terlingua and the water had come down the creek in a yellow flood. It had spread out over the valley and irrigated all the little farms, and men,

women, and children were out feverishly cutting
ditches, building *borditos* (levees), and planting crops.
El Piocho rubbed his bleary eyes, took a good look,
and shouted for his teamsters.

"*Ahora sí! Muchachos*, there is water. Bring in the
oxen: Let us go. *Vámonos! Andale!*"

He was surprised and enraged when he found that
the two bridegrooms had no intention of going with
him. "If you please me, *Señor!* The crops are planted.
We must stay and help the Old One and the *mujercitas*
(young ladies) or there will be no food this winter."

El Piocho might have reminded them that the Old
One and the mujercitas had gotten along very well before they came. Instead, it seems that he tried to force
them to go, but the villagers sided with the boys and
raised enough money to pay El Piocho what he claimed
the boys owed him. They insinuated to the angry *capitán* that it would be better if he moved on. They per-
suaded or forced a couple of worthless half-Indian
boys, who lived mostly by stealing and begging to re-
place the balking teamsters, thus at once getting rid of
the thieving lads and the now raging El Piocho.

Although the new teamsters were nearly worthless,
the train made good progress for a few days, until
someone killed a black-tailed deer for meat. The two
half-breeds sat up nearly all night, cooking and eating
meat, and next morning there wasn't enough of that

deer left to feed a kitten, while the boys, with distended stomachs, were snoring under one of the carretas. When they were kicked awake, they merely wriggled a little farther under the carreta and went to sleep again.

The terrible-tempered El Piocho had the other teamsters drag them out while he tried to flog them with a big rawhide whip, but the slippery half-breeds squirmed free and made off in the brush and could not be found, no doubt glad to get away from this *loco* who insisted on a fellow working when he wasn't even hungry. (Old Tío's account of this was very humorous and quite unprintable.)

So the harried *capitán* left the train camped and rode off in search of new teamsters. Old Tío didn't know where—maybe to Terlingua, maybe to San Carlos or Presidio. He brought back two, and one of them was an extraordinarily capable man. Not only was he a good *carretero* (cart driver) and a skilled plainsman, but he also knew the country and the location of water, grass, and trails, and he spoke several Indian languages or dialects.

El Piocho was congratulating himself on getting this man, when they camped near an Indian village. The Indians were friendly enough until they saw the new teamster. Then they pointed and muttered *"Comanchero,"* also his Indian name, and other names even less complimentary. It seems that this man had once lived with the Comanches, and according to these Indians, who were Apaches, he had committed numerous atrocities against their people.

The Apaches were great guerrilla fighters, as shown by their exploits under Geronimo and other chieftains. The Comanches were not only good at guerrilla tactics, they were also terrible in open battle, so every time the Apache warriors fought against them, the Apaches got their pants licked off. Consequently, they hated the Comanches almost as much as they hated the Gringos and Mexicans. They would have eliminated the newcomer on the spot, but El Piocho and the others interfered and drove the sullen and muttering Indians away.

From then on the trip was a nightmare. That very night the oxen were stampeded and an attempt was made to kill the *comanchero*. Most of the oxen were recovered next day and the train moved on, but the Indians harried them every step of the way. From ambush they shot arrows into the oxen, so that the poor beasts died or became unfit for work. At night they sneaked up and shot blazing arrows into the carretas, setting them on fire. The teamsters got afraid to graze the oxen at night, and the Indians burned off the country so that there was no grass for them even in the daytime.

In spite of his drunkenness and uncontrollable temper, El Piocho must have been a man of courage and resolution. He could, no doubt, have ended all this by giving up the *comanchero* to the Indians, but he hung on and beat off attack after attack, so that things went from bad to worse. Evidently he gave up trying to reach his destination and tried to go back by another route. As the story goes, some months after the train had left Chihuahua, they got back to Terlingua with only one carreta, two oxen, and what was left of the teamsters, most of them wounded and all weary and scared.

El Piocho was ruined. Not only had he lost his own capital, but it seems he also had lost the confidence of the merchants who backed him in his enterprises. Probably he lost his nerve as well. Always a hearty drinker, he apparently took up drinking as a career from then on. Old Tío said that when he was a boy he knew this El Piocho, then an old man and drunken bum, though he had once been a noted *capitán* and trader with the Indians. When he could get liquor he would get drunk and tell of his past greatness, and would cry and curse and bring down the maledictions of heaven on the two men who had left him for their brides and the life of a farmer. He blamed them for all his trouble.

And the boys and their brides? And the village? Old Tío said he didn't know. When he was a young man,

Indians were pretty bad in that country. He mostly went on long trips to San Antonio and Santa Fé, and did not see Terlingua until after the Indians were driven out. Then he found it looking pretty much as his grandfather had described it. He thought maybe the settlers left the valley for a while because of Indian raids and came back to it when the Indians were finally driven away.

The old man's account was rambling and disconnected, and he admitted that his memory was not clear about a good many things. But Tío was an ignorant *peón* who could not read or write and had neither the knowledge nor the imagination to have concocted such a tale out of thin air. It interested me so that I have remembered it all these years and write it as I heard it.

Years later I heard various things that partly confirmed his stories. One was from an old Mexican woman living in Marfa who claimed to be more than one hundred years old. She said that when she was a little girl, her people were settlers near the mouth of Terlingua Creek. She said the country still belonged to Spain, and that they finally had to leave "because the Indians and rattlesnakes were so bad."

El Cíbolo and the Indians

The stories of El Cíbolo are from two different men, who, I believe, never met. Both are told as complete stories and translated from the Spanish, almost word for word, as I remember them. I understand that one has been published—with widely differing details. There are other, incomplete stories of this legendary character. One says El Cíbolo lived for a time in the Big Bend, that Cíbolo Creek in south Presidio County was named for him. He was over six feet tall, so dark and with such a mop of black, kinky hair that he appeared to have Negro blood. On account of this shaggy, kinky mop like a buffalo's poll, he was called *"El Cíbolo,"* and it seems to be a fact that the Apaches called the Negro soldiers *cíbolos* (buffaloes) for the same reason.

El Cíbolo was a man of Herculean or Paul Bunyan-like prowess on the Chihuahua Trail.[1] He seems to

[1] The Chihuahua Trail went from Chihuahua, Mexico, down the Conchos River to Ojinaga (in early days called Presidio del Norte), where it crossed the Río Grande. It ascended Alamito Creek, went through Paisano Pass to Comanche Spring (now Fort Stockton). Wagons crossed the Pecos River at Horsehead Crossing (in Crane County) or at Fort Lancaster (now Sheffield). The trail then went down the Devil's River to San Felipe (now Del Rio), and eastward to San Antonio.

have been a pretty tough bird, something of a renegade and near bandit. He sold liquor and weapons to the Indians and would have them steal or kill for him when he thought it necessary. He must have been a thorn in the side of the authorities, who always had enough trouble keeping down the Indians anyway. Nevertheless, the men who worked for him as teamsters would gladly have died for him and no white man in the country had more control over the wild Indians than he. This story tells something of how he dealt with Indians who crossed him.

He kept a *campo de remonte* (remount camp) somewhere in what is now Presidio County in the Big Bend. There he kept his extra teams and saddle stock, and every four to six months he would pass by this camp and get fresh animals, turn loose to grass the tired, thin, footsore animals that had been working steadily for some months, and go on about his business. He had men who did nothing but herd these animals.

Most wagon trains passing through the Indian country used oxen, because, as one old teamster explained to me, although the Indians might kill one for meat once in a while, or kill several for pure cussedness, they never could drive them off very fast or very far. The Indians soon learned this, and no longer tried to steal oxen. The bold Cíbolo, however, had no fear of Indians, and used mule teams. He also had some of the finest and fastest saddle horses anywhere in the country.

On one occasion he had loaded his wagons with trade goods, changed to fresh teams and had gone toward the staked plains. Arriving at the village of a chief, a friend of his, El Cíbolo gave the chief some presents. The next thing in order was a buffalo hunt to get meat for a big feast and pow-wow.

Practically the entire male population went on the hunt. When they returned the next day, loaded with buffalo meat, they found that during their absence a band of roving Indians had raided the village, set fire to everything that would burn, looted El Cíbolo's wagons, and killed one of his teamsters, and another teamster had an arrow through his arm. They had driven off all the stock, including El Cíbolo's teams. Squaws and children, many of them wounded, were still crawling out of the bushes where they had hidden.

Being already armed and mounted, El Cíbolo and his friends at once set out in pursuit. They soon overtook the raiders who, Indian fashion, were carrying all their loot on the horses they were riding, though they must have been driving a hundred head of stock that would have served for pack animals. This proved to be their undoing, as their loaded horses were already tired. The raiders were too outnumbered to make a fight, so they began to throw away their loads and run for it.

El Cíbolo's horse was much faster than any of those the Indians rode, so he soon overtook them with his own yipping band strung out like trailing hounds behind. Riding a little to one side nearly out of arrow range, and reloading at a gallop after the fashion of the old buffalo hunters, El Cíbolo shot the Indians from their running ponies, as a skilled hunter shoots quail on the wing. If an Indian hung on the opposite side of his horse, leaving only his foot and forearm exposed, El Cíbolo shot the horse, leaving the rider afoot and at the mercy of the howling pack that came on behind. Some of them left the bunch like locoed steers and struck out for themselves. Some jumped from their tiring horses and tried to hide in the low bushes. El Cíbolo paid no attention to these. He knew his friends, coming up fast now, would hunt them down like hound-dogs hunt a fox. So he kept on after the main bunch, and kept knocking them down until only one was left, the leader, whose horse was now stumbling and staggering.

The Indian flogged his failing horse with his tomahawk, using even the cutting edge, but the horse soon came to a stop, his feet outspread, his heart drumming his ribs and his breath whistling through his throat, literally dying on his feet, as horses of wild Indians nearly always died.

The Indian looked back. His pursuer was coming at

a slow trot, and he no doubt thought the other horse
was also spent, for he started to run on foot. But his
relentless pursuer came on. Always crowding him into
running his best but never coming close enough to
make him lose hope and stand and fight, El Cíbolo
literally ran the heart out of the Indian, and after a
mile or so he was going at just a weary trot. He tried to
turn off right to a little brushy draw, but El Cíbolo
galloped up and headed him away from it, just as a
skilled cowhand heads a calf in the way it should go.

The Indian knew then that the game was up, so he
stopped and tried to die fighting like a warrior, but he
was too weary even to raise his tomahawk. El Cíbolo
took him prisoner and marched him back until they
met the jubilant and victorious Indians. They at once
began to plan things to do to the prisoner but El Cíbolo
intervened, saying that the prisoner was his and he
should be allowed to do as he liked with him. The Indians agreed, so El Cíbolo spoke to his captive.

"Listen," he said, "I could have killed you many
times over, but I have left you to carry word to your
people and to other people beyond yours, so listen well
to what I have to say.

"I am El Cíbolo. I am a friend to the Indians. I
bring them presents. I trade fairly with them, but you
and your men have killed my servants, burned my
wagons, stolen my animals and goods.

"Go, then, and tell all people, whenever you meet them, that what has happened to you and your men shall happen to all those who do not carry themselves well with El Cíbolo." He took a string of buffalo meat from his saddle and tossed it to the Indian. "Take this. Now go! *Anda vete!* (Go see to that!)"

The Indian slunk away in the gathering dusk, and from that day on, no Indian in all West Texas and New Mexico ever bothered El Cíbolo or his men or anything that was his.

El Cíbolo and the Spaniards

The following is a Mexican version of a story that has been printed in English. Although differing greatly in places, it is undoubtedly the same story, and is either about the same man or about two men whose identities were confused because they had the same nicknames. One very noticeable difference is that in the English version it is stated that El Cíbolo's mother and sister were with him when he was captured, and were abused by the Spanish officers.

Well, maybe so, but I have always noticed that in connection with the tough characters like, for instance, Billy the Kid or Pancho Villa, there is always a story that he killed his first man or started his career as an outlaw in defense of some female member of his family. This not only puts a little heart interest into the story but also enlists the sympathy of people who might otherwise denounce said character as a bloodthirsty so-and-so.

Be that as it may, I relate the story as I remember hearing it.

It was early spring when El Cíbolo's wagons pulled out of his old camp in the Big Bend. The wagons all were loaded with things to trade to the Indians. The mules were fat, and as they stepped out briskly the little bells on their harness jingled in harmony. El Cíbolo rode in the lead, as usual, on one of his best horses.

They drove north slightly by east. They probably passed where old Fort Davis was later established and down Limpia Canyon. They struck the Pecos River and continued up it far into New Mexico. This was not a continuous journey. Long stops were made in Indian villages and trading was brisk. As the stock of trade goods went down, the stock of buffalo hides and furs rose correspondingly.

Finally, by easy stages they found themselves far up in New Mexico. Just where, I either have forgotten or was not told.

Anyhow they were somewhere near a fort garrisoned by a troop commanded by Spanish officers. When a detachment of soldiers in the charge of a *teniente* (lieutenant) came out and told El Cíbolo to report to the *comandante,* he went readily enough. On other occasions he had been hailed before the authorities and had paid a stiff fine which was really a bribe, but on this occasion he no sooner entered the fort than he was seized and put in chains. Later his teams, wagons, and all that was in them were brought into the fort.

The *comandante* then informed El Cíbolo that his property had been seized by the authorities and that he was to be sent to Mexico City in chains. Somewhere on the way or maybe even before leaving the fort, El Cíbolo knew, he would be "shot while trying to escape."

Even if he should get away with a whole skin he was ruined. Nearly all he had in the world was tied up in fine teams and wagons and the goods were on them. Except for the extra animals left back in the Big Bend, all he had in the world was in the hands of the Spaniards.

He looked the fort over carefully. He noted the buildings, the stockade, the location of the sentries. He saw how easy it would be for a band of determined fighting men, properly instructed and led, to capture this fort. If he could only manage to escape!

There had been quite a lot of liquor in the wagons, and the *comandante,* with unusual generosity, had issued some of it to the soldiers. All the officers were drunk, including the *comandante*, who reeled around to where El Cíbolo was chained, to tell him how low an opinion he had of him and what he aimed to do to him.

The soldiers, too, were all drunk except the ones on guard, and an unusually big, ugly fellow was guarding El Cíbolo. He engaged the guard in conversation and told him what a shame it was that nearly everybody should be having a good time while he and a few others should have to be on guard, carrying heavy muskets and bayonets. The guard agreed heartily.

"Listen," said the wily trader. "In a little box underneath the lead wagon is a bottle of very fine liquor I keep for my own use. Go and get it and we will both have a drink." It was now getting dark, so the guard did as he was told and soon he was very drunk. El Cíbolo pretended to be drunk, and soon each was telling the other how strong he was.

"Why," said the trader, "I can take an iron bar in my teeth and my two hands and bend it double."

The guard doubted that it could be done, so he went and got a thick iron bar to prove that he was right. Whereupon El Cíbolo whacked the bibulous and trusting soldier on the head, after which he pried the chains loose from the wall. In the blacksmith shop, which he had previously located, he got them off of his ankles.

He met an Indian stalking on the guard at the stables and laid him out. Then, after dealing likewise with the sentry at the gate, he saddled his horse and rode away.

He rode east toward Texas, and after days of hard riding was back among the Indians he was looking for. The story does not state what Indians these were. They were probably Comanches, as they were said to be the best fighters and were always ready to take a jab at Mexicans and Spaniards.

El Cíbolo carefully picked the best men and horses. During the trip back to New Mexico, they traveled only at night and hid in the daytime, lest word get to the fort of their approach. The surprise attack was made at night, and the fort was captured in one quick rush. The sentries were pierced with arrows before they could give the alarm. Most of the officers were killed in their night clothes before they could get to their weapons. If El Cíbolo had intended only to get his stuff back without slaughtering the garrison, he must have lost control of his Indians, for the story says that hardly a man escaped, and before dawn the fort was looted and burning until it burned to the ground.

El Cíbolo knew that after this he would be an outlaw and would never be safe in Spanish territory again, so he loaded his Indian allies with loot and sent them back. Then he loaded his wagons high with everything valuable and left, going toward the north.

No one knows where he went. He never returned to his team camp in the Big Bend, and he sent back the teamsters who lived in Presidio and Chihuahua. One of the teamsters told something of this story to his grandson, who was past eighty in 1913.

2. Romance in a Wigwam

Maybe it was not exactly a wigwam, if you are thinking about those snug, conical affairs you see pictured. The Big Bend Indians didn't build them quite according to those specifications. In the summer they just pulled the tops of some bushes together and tied them, and maybe threw some extra brush around in the openest places. Sometimes a hide or two was put up, to knock off the worst of the rain. Although their winter quarters were more elaborate, they were still a bit shy of the luxuriousness of a Fifth Avenue penthouse.

These winter lodges were started by laying a nearly

complete circle of rocks on the ground. The circle was usually eight to ten feet in diameter and sometimes the rocks would be built up to a low wall a foot or so in height. Next, poles were set up with the bottoms braced against the rocks, and the tops of the poles were tied together. Then brush, skins, and what-have-you would cover the poles. A hole was left for a door, and this, almost without exception, opened toward the southeast. Another hole was left at the top for the smoke to get out, and while the squaws carried brush for firewood, Big Chief sat by the fire and sat and sat.

There were probably a good many variations of this model, but judging from the descriptions I have heard of them, as well as remains of them I have seen in old Indian camps, this was the usual setup. Since this event happened around one hundred years ago, I guess this was the kind of residence in which this particular Indian—"What Indian?" sez you, rousing for a moment from your nap. "And what was he particular about?" you further inquire.

Sure enough, as usual, I've been telling my story without either beginning or end, just sort of a casual stroll among the details, you might say, but as long as I've frittered away so much time, I might as well keep frittering, until I've said my say.

As I was about to say, the wild Indians and the more-or-less tame Mexicans lived almost side by side in the

Big Bend for generations—and unless you insist on counting stealing, cheating, and plain and fancy bushwhacking, they got along very well. They did not mingle socially to any great extent. Though the Mexicans were themselves part Indian, their ancestors had mostly been civilized for possibly as long as the Spaniards had, and they did not, as a rule, fraternize or intermarry with the wild Indians.

There were exceptions, of course. It is said that some of the old traders, who spent most of their time with Indians anyhow, had a squaw in every village. There were men who settled in remote districts and married squaws. However, the term "squaw-man" carried the same social stigma in Spanish that it did in English, and this was perhaps no more common among the Mexicans than among the English-speaking people.

I have heard of instances where Indian children, both boys and girls, were adopted by Mexican families who raised them as their own, and these children grew up and married among the Mexican boys and girls without arousing special comment. But for a well-raised Mexican girl to marry a wild Indian was unusual and something of a scandal. The old Mexican women along the Río Grande still tell, with shocked amusement, various versions of this story.

This girl we'll call María, since that's short and easy to remember. She grew up in an ordinary and unspectacular way, and married a boy we'll call José, for short and handy. He had hardly more than a walk-on part in this "drammer," so I can't give you many details about him. He probably farmed a little patch with burros or oxen, and maybe he also had a few goats, pigs, and chickens. Anyhow, after a couple of years or so with him, María suddenly left him and their one child, and went to live with a wild Indian, and all efforts of her family and of José to get her to come back were of no avail. She maintained, to the last, that she went of her own free will and was not frightened or coerced in any way, nor would she say why she had preferred the Indian to José.

The "loaf of bread, jug of wine, and thou singing in the wilderness" idea hardly applied here. María certainly had the wilderness and the thou, but if there was any bread in that brush shack, she must have brought it with her. There may have been an occasional jug of wine that found its way there; but as for giving a squaw any of it—perish the thought, and the thought would have to perish darn fast to have done so before the wine did. Indians had the idea that liquor was made to be drunk, and they acted accordingly. They say that the rpm of an Indian's Adam's apple, when properly accelerated by *aguardiente* flowing over his tonsils, was only a few beats shy of that of the wing of a hummingbird in full flight.

And if there was any singing in that wilderness, it must have been done by the coyotes. Indians, on rare occasions, did what was called singing—war songs or death songs, for instance—but was mostly discordant screeching. Personally I'd prefer the coyotes. Like most Mexican girls, María probably had been brought up to sing in harmony with other girls, but there was nobody to harmonize with here.

She probably found other things different, too. At home she had a *metate* and a *mano* for grinding corn. A *metate*, in case you don't know, is a piece of rock about 12 by 14 inches, nicely shaped and hollowed with Aztec skill. A *mano* is a fist-size rock, curved to fit the curve of the metate. María soaked the corn in water overnight, and ground it in the metate with a sort of rubbing motion with the mano. After it was crushed into a kind of paste it was cooked in thin cakes, usually on a piece of sheet iron, over live coals. These cakes, again in case you don't know their name, were called *tortillas*.

The Indians didn't have those nicely shaped metates and manos. María probably had a crude *molino*, a rock which would have taken two men to lift, if there had ever been occasion to lift it. This rock was crudely hollowed out for a depth of a few inches and the mano was most any shape or size rock handy, provided it had one smooth and rounded side, and if they had ever had any corn to grind, you could be sure it had been stolen or obtained by some means from the Mexicans.

What María had to grind in that molino, most of the time, was probably the beans of the mesquite, cat-claw, and *tornillo*, and various wild seeds of one kind or another. The squaws laboriously ground mesquite beans in those crude molinos into a pasty, gooey kind of stuff which was then put in a hollow rock or hollow log and allowed to harden. And harden it did, almost to the consistency of concrete. They say it wasn't bad eating, if your dental equipment was equal to the task. When game or other food was scarce, the Indians would live almost entirely on this and roasted *sotol*.

Ever see a *sotol?* If you can imagine a plant with the inside something like a very fibrous cabbagehead, and protected on the outside by an assortment of two-edged saws with hooked teeth, that's something like it.

When María's lord and master wanted roasted sotol for dinner, she had first to catch her sotol. She would take a squaw-ax, which is a flat flint rock with one sharp edge and a stick tied on with rawhide for a handle. It was nothing like the fancy tomahawks the braves used, but was good enough for a squaw. She would climb a mountainside until she found a likely sotol and hack away its two-edged saw blades until only the head was left, looking something like an overgrown pineapple. This she would lug down the mountain. When she got back to the village the other squaws probably had copped all the wood handy, so she had to trudge a half mile or so and carry back a load of wood. She then built a fire and threw in a lot of small rocks. When the fire was burned down to a lot of coals, hot rocks, and ashes, she would bury the sotol head in this and leave it there until it was well done, rare, or medium, as her brave preferred. At home she would have had a big adobe oven to roast or bake in, and it probably would have been a *calabaza* instead of a sotol head. No, she didn't sit down and watch that sotol head roast, either. There were skins to be made into buckskin, later to be made into leggings and moccasins. And when her lord and master was around, he always had to be waited on.

Maybe, after all, María didn't weaken. Maybe there was something else. He might have gotten tired of her because she would not bring his bedroom moccasins and pipe every night. She might have gotten sore because he made eyes at other copper-colored cuties, or there may have been mental cruelty on one side or the other. At any rate, the disease caused by the virus from Cupid's arrow is violent, but seldom fatal, and, glory be, not always chronic. So one night, about two years after the wife of his bosom had left him, José sat by candlelight in his little house. There was a scratching at the door.

"*Quién vive?*" he challenged.

The scratching continued. He opened the door and peered cautiously out. There stood María with a half-Indian tot strapped, squaw fashion, to her back.

"*Ya volví,*" she said.

"*Pase, pues,*" said he.

Just like that! No "I've done you wrong," no "Come to my arms, all is forgiven," or stuff like that. Just "I've come back" and "Come in, then."

They say he raised the half-breed Indian child as his own. It grew up, married, raised children, and, in due course of time, went the way of all flesh. Some of this half-Indian child's descendants still live in the Big Bend, a fact which they neither boast of nor deny.

3. Places, Names, and What Happened

El Cerro Santiago

antiago Mountain is a prominent feature of the Big Bend. Situated about the center of Brewster County, Texas' largest county, it can be seen from all adjoining counties as well as from some points in Mexico. It is nearly 7,000 feet above sea level and more than half that above the surrounding country.

Its name is a very common one among Spanish-speaking people. Santiago (or Santo Yago or San Diego) was the patron saint of the Spanish Military Order of Santiago, and his name was the battle cry of all Spanish warriors as they went into action. Throughout the Spanish-speaking world there are people and places named for this ancient and honored saint, and it would seem that this mountain was named in his honor also. However, there are various stories which account for its name.

I first heard one version from a Mexican called Old Méndez. His first name was Prejádis. He had served as a soldier under Benito Juárez, and claimed that as a cavalryman guarding the area, he had witnessed the execution of the Emperor Maximilian on the *Cerro de las Campañas* near the city of Puebla in 1867, an event well known to readers of history. Afterwards he was sent to Juárez and from there to Presidio del Norte (now Ojinaga, Mexico, and Presidio, Texas). I have since learned that the garrison at Ojinaga, in those days, consisted mostly of *presidiales*, or convict soldiers.

The first version, told by old Méndez, goes something like this: Santiago was born in Mexico of pure Spanish blood. At the time of this story he lived at the fort and frontier settlement of Presidio del Norte. Apparently he had no official position, but he was held in great respect by all, including the wild Indians. These last had at that time raided an outlying settlement, killed a few settlers, and made off with some stock. Santiago and some of his neighbors organized a small force and started in pursuit, hoping to recover the stock and avenge the deaths of their friends.

After a few days they overtook the Indians, who charged the small force at once. At the first attack, Santiago's comrades all fled. They were all peaceful farmers who had never known battle, but Santiago stayed and fought alone. He was a natural fighter, because his father, whose sword he now carried and which he had sworn never to disgrace, had been a famous Spanish soldier.

After his firearms were empty, he stayed and fought with his father's sword. However, this unequal combat could have only one ending. Pierced by many arrows, both he and his horse went down to rise no more.

As he lay dying, pinned down by his fallen horse, he wept with rage and frustration at his helplessness and at the cowardice of his comrades. The Indians, who knew him well, tried to console him by telling him he had killed more of their party than they had of his own. This must have been small consolation to Santiago, since he was the one killed and the only one who stayed and fought.

Old Méndez did not mention Santiago Mountain, but his story of the brave Santiago is something like a second version I later read in a book called *Romance of Davis Mountains and Big Bend Country*.[1] The book

[1] Carlysle Graham Raht, *The Romance of Davis Mountains and Big Bend Country*, The Rahtbooks Co., El Paso, 1919, pp. 80–81.

version of this story says that the battle took place at
the foot of Santiago Mountain and that the mountain
was named for this Santiago. Another version of the
story says that Santiago was not killed at the foot of
Santiago Mountain, but at Puerto Potrillo, a mountain
gap, which, though in sight of the mountain, is some
twenty-five or thirty miles to the west. The Indians
traveling from Presidio to the heart of the Indian
country in the Big Bend would have been likely to pass
through that gap.

There are at least two more stories that account for
the name of Santiago Mountain. The third story I heard
from a scholarly eccentric called *"El Santo."* I never
knew his real name. His version antedates the others by
at least a century, to about 1750 anyway. It relates that
a small band of Spanish soldiers was passing near, or
at least in sight of, this mountain, the top of which was
hidden this day by clouds. The Spaniards were suddenly confronted by hostile Indians many times their
number. The soldiers were dismayed, but their leader
rallied them by reminding them that their patron saint
had always watched over them.

"Even now," he said, "he may be watching from the
clouds on yonder mountain!"

Whereupon the soldiers, shouting their battle cry of
"Santiago! *Sanuago!*" charged with such fury that the
Indians were scattered like chaff before the wind.

The fourth version is built up from fragmentary and casual remarks from several sources. This story tells of a happening probably in the 1860's or 1870's, since it is stated that it took place only a short time before the Indians were rounded up for keeps. In the 1920's there were still old Mexicans around San Carlos who took part in it.

The little town of San Carlos is about twelve miles south of the Río Grande in the state of Chihuahua, and is about one hundred and twenty miles south of Alpine, Texas. At the time of this story, Indians often came to San Carlos to trade, drink, and gamble. They were great gamblers, and one old Mexican woman still living in San Carlos tells of dealing monte to Indians when she was a very young girl, being unusually deft with cards. They usually lost everything they had and nearly always raised a little cane before they left.

On this occasion a band of Indians had ridden into San Carlos from across the border. Their chief was named Santiago and was known to be a bad actor, so as soon as the citizens saw him they began to get ready for trouble. The Indians hung around the town a few days, no doubt trading, gambling, and drinking when they could get liquor. The wary townsmen watched and were ready.

Then suddenly it happened. The Indians *pegaron unos gritos* (cut loose with war whoops) and began to shoot up the town. One story says that they carried off some captives, including some young girls, and that Santiago dragged one girl down the street by her long hair before lifting her on his horse, all the while yelling defiance at the citizens who were trying to rescue the poor girl. Indians did sometimes steal Mexican girls, and something of the kind must have happened to rouse the Mexicans to such a fighting fury.

At any rate, the Indians were hardly clear of the town before the Mexicans were in hot pursuit. The Mexicans were well armed and were mounted on well-fed, rested horses, whereas the Indians' ponies probably hadn't had anything at all to eat while their masters were hanging around town. Therefore, before the Indians reached the river their pursuers overtook them, and a running battle followed which lasted the rest of the day and took them far into the Big Bend in Texas. All the Indians were killed except Santiago, who, probably being better mounted than the others, got away in the darkness.

At dawn the vengeful Mexicans took up his trail, and followed the tracks of his weary horse northward. Late in the evening they sighted him approaching the tall lone mountain, which must be sixty or seventy miles from San Carlos.

"*Ahora sí!*" they called to each other, and began to fan out to surround the rider and horse now barely able to trot. But Santiago abandoned the horse and clambered up the rough mountainside where being on foot was an advantage, and he managed to elude his pursuers until night.

As darkness fell, he taunted them from among the rocks.

"*Soy Santiago!*" he would yell—"I am Santiago!" —following with a stream of broken and obscene Spanish and boasts in his native Indian tongue.

The next morning no trace of him could be found. He had gotten clean away and presumably was killed or captured in the big roundup of Indians that took place shortly afterwards.

El Caballo Muerto

As you approach the Chisos Mountains from the north over Texas State Highway 227, you see on your left a high gray limestone backbone running roughly northwest-southeast and apparently ending against the cliffs of the Del Carmens across the river. This is Dead Horse Mountain.[2] Mexicans usually call it *Caballo Muerto*, which is a pretty good sign that the mountain has had this name a long time. There is also Dead

[2] The National Park Service signs now designate this landmark as "Dagger Mountain."

Horse Canyon running parallel with this mountain and emptying into the Río Grande. This canyon is named either for the mountain or vice versa.

It has been claimed that the canyon, though at present known by that name, is not the original Dead Horse Canyon. But more of that later. As to why mountain and canyon are called by this peculiar name, the generally accepted story goes something like this:

There was once a bunch of Texas Rangers going up (or down) the Río Grande, some say, in a boat. They encountered a band of Indians with some horses at the river's edge. They probably were just some boys watering or otherwise taking care of the horses, for it seems they didn't put up a fight but abandoned the horses and scattered into the brush.

The Rangers of course knew that if they left the horses the Indians would come back and get them, and these same horses would be used to raid settlements and fight white men. So they killed all the horses and went on their way. Tradition says this took place at the mouth of the canyon and the nearby mountain.[3]

[3] Other versions include those in Ross A. Maxwell, "Big Bend National Park, a Land of Contrasts," *Big Bend Park Issue* (West Texas Historical and Scientific Society Publication No. 12), Sul Ross State Teachers College Bulletin, Vol. XXVIII, No. 2 (June 1, 1948), p. 11; and Virginia Madison, *The Big Bend Country,* The University of New Mexico Press, Albuquerque, 1955, pp. 25–26.

The second story, as another interesting tale, gives a different reason for the naming of Dead Horse Mountain.

It was in the early 1880's, when two cowmen were making their way toilsomely through the tangled hills and canyons on the Texas side of the Río Grande, opposite the towering cliffs of the Del Carmens. They may have been hunting strayed animals. More than likely they were just exploring to see what the country looked like. As to who these two men were, there seems to be some difference of opinion. As nearly all the old timers, who might know for certain, are now riding the Celestial Ranges, it might be best to just call the two cowmen "They."

"They" looked down from the rim of a box canyon on the Río Grande, and saw some fifteen or twenty horses imprisoned within the canyon walls. They were not mustangs but saddle horses, with saddle and cinch marks showing plainly on their backs and bellies, and some of them wore Mexican brands. How the horses had gotten into this canyon was a mystery, as the two white men could find no trail where they could have descended. The river was blocked above and below them by rapids and boulders so that it looked impossible for the horses to cross. It seems likely that either Indians or Mexican horse thieves had gotten the horses into this canyon by some means or other, possibly by

Trapper McMahon, early-day Big Bend trapper, with a load of bobcat hides.

Sierra del Carmen escarpment in Mexico with buildings in the village of Boquillas in the foreground. Shot Tower is seen in the distance to the left. (Photograph by George A. Grant)

Jail in Boquillas, Mexico. (Photograph by George A. Grant)

The Rio Grande from Boquillas, Mexico, showing the Chisos Mountains in the distance in Texas. (Photograph by George A. Grant)

Boquillas Canyon between Sierra del Terminal and the high Sierra del Carmen escarpment.

Boquillas flagstone near San Vincente Mountain, Big Bend National Park.

Small canyon in the Rio Grande above Rio Grande Village, Big Bend National Park.

Sierra Ponce in Mexico from between Castolon and Johnson's ranch on the Río Grande. (Photograph by George A. Grant)

Punta de la Sierra, the southern point of the Chisos Mountains, taken from near Johnson's ranch.

Aerial view of Santa Elena Canyon; Mesa de Anguila (Texas) on the
right, Sierra Ponce (Mexico) on the left.

The interior of Santa Elena Canyon.

Cemetery at Lajitas, Texas. (Photograph by George A. Grant)

Badland topography along the Río Grande, south of Lajitas, Texas.

Igneous intrusion in limestone formation on U.S. Highway 385, about thirty miles south of Marathon.

Casa Grande in the Basin of the Chisos Mountains. (Photograph by George A. Grant)

Looking northward from South Rim of the Chisos Mountains (*in right corner*). Mountain on the left is adjacent to Blue Creek Canyon.

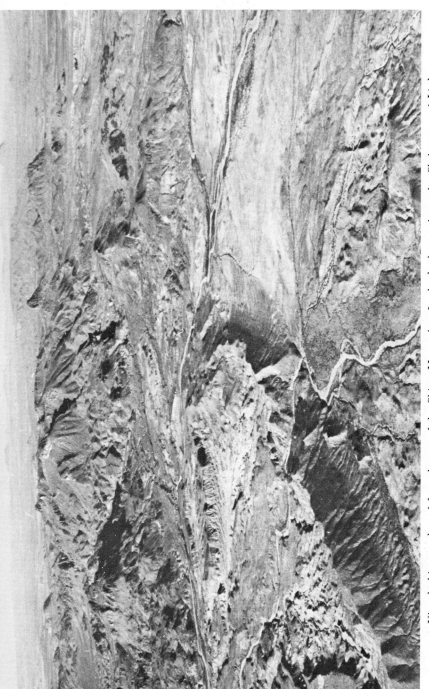

View looking northward from the top of the Chisos Mountains. In the background are the Christmas and Little Christmas mountains; Santiago Peak is on the skyline to the right.

Cow Heaven Anticline, Elephant Tusk, and South Rim of the Chisos Mountains (*in background*).

Aguja sandstone ledges, Big Bend National Park.

Vertical rocks in Dog Canyon, Big Bend National Park.

swimming them in at high water or by picking their way in at extremely low water, only to find later that they couldn't get them out. And maybe for some reason ˋ they just never returned for them.

The two cowmen made several attempts to get the horses out of their canyon prison, going down on ropes to explore the canyon on foot, in hopes of finding a way out. Although they had no luck at this, they kept going back for several months. They would go each time they could get off from their work, but the horses, having eaten all the vegetation within those confining walls, finally began to starve to death. One day the two men looked down from the rim to see a few skeletons scattered here and there, all that was left of what may have been somebody's *remuda.* So they called it "Dead Horse Canyon" and called the mountain that abutted on the river at or near this place by the same name.

As to why the present Dead Horse Canyon is called by that name instead of the canyon where the horses died, I have heard this story: Some twenty or more years after the event just narrated, a group of explorers, surveyors, map makers, geologists, or some such *gente,* for some reason wanted to go to the Dead Horse Canyon. They hired a local man as guide and packer. As there was, and still is, no wagon road, everything had to be carried in on mules or burros. Now the canyon where the horses died is in the most remote and inaccessible part of the country. At the end of the first day out, after changing to pack animals, they arrived at the canyon now known as Dead Horse.

When the local man was plumb wore out and disgusted with answering fool questions and with packing all the tents, mattresses, cots, and other paraphernalia these tenderfeet seemed to think necessary for a little camping trip, he just told them, "This is it."

And so it appeared on the map and so it is to this day. Then again, this mountain, like many others, may have been named back in the days of the Spanish explorers. A dead horse in those days, with a fellow's second best horse somewhere down about Mexico City or maybe clear across the Atlantic in Spain, would have been a major disaster, and an event well worth naming a mountain for.[4]

However, a few old-time Mexicans scoff at all these stories. They say the mountains, the canyon, and the region in general were the old Comanche Trail, which was so named because of the hundreds of whitening skeletons of horses the Comanches always left behind, since their custom was to ride a horse to death and then

[4] Larence Hardin of Crane, Texas, has heard that during a drouth, ranchers once moved their horses onto this mountain, where grass stood belly deep. Then when the horses starved of thirst by the hundreds, the mountain was named "Dead Horse Mountain."

eat him. This also sounds reasonable to me. Take your choice.

That Word "Chisos"

The Chisos Mountains are the most prominent feature of the entire Big Bend country. Standing around 8,000 feet above sea level and covered with timber in the midst of a barren desert land, they drew the attention of the early Spaniards, and are still the major attraction for visitors to the Big Bend National Park. Naturally a great many stories have grown up around them. The most prominent of these is of the Lost Chisos Mine, for which hopeful prospectors have been searching the past century or longer.

Any repetition of some of these oft-told tales would be a waste of time and paper. My main object in writing this chapter is to shoot holes in a story that has for some time gained wide credence but that to me is pure bunk.

That is the idea that the word *chisos* means "ghost."

This idea is the theme of the story of Alsate (or Arzate), the Apache chief who, legend says, made his way on foot from Yucatán back to his home in northern Mexico and the Texas Big Bend, a distance of more than a thousand miles. Story says he hid for a time in the Chisos Mountains. His presence there led to the belief that the mountains were haunted, hence the name *chisos* meaning "ghost."[5]

When I first encountered this yarn, it was supposed and stated that the word *chisos* was Spanish, but this was easily disproved. Now it is stated that it is an Indian word meaning "ghost." The language of the Apaches who inhabited the Big Bend was at one time known to a great many people. I have heard certain clicks, grunts, and sneezes said to be the Apache way of referring to a disembodied spirit. None of them sounded like *chisos*. The Apaches were very superstitious and saw ghosts in everything, so their word for ghost was fairly well known.

After some thirty years of listening, reading, and thinking, I have come to the conclusion that the word cannot mean "ghost" for these reasons: First, as far as I have been able to find out after years of study, *chisos* does not mean "ghost" in any known language, living or dead. Second, the idea is wrapped up with the story of Alsate, whose prime was in the 1870's and '80's, and the mountains were certainly called Chisos long

[5] See Raht, *The Romance of Davis Mountains and Big Bend Country*, pp. 277–279; Virginia Madison and Hallie Stillwell, *How Come It's Called That? Place Names in the Big Bend Country*, University of New Mexico Press, Albuquerque, 1958, pp. 27–30; Elton Miles, "Chisos Ghosts," in Mody C. Boatright *et al.* (eds.), *Madstones and Twisters*, Southern Methodist University Press, Dallas, 1958, pp. 106–122.

before then. Third, all the stories of Alsate are so varied and contradictory that none of them can be relied upon. Fourth, at the time of Alsate's return, there were no Indians to give the mountains an Indian name. Any name given to them at this time would have been more likely to be Spanish or English.

There are other theories of which these people who accept the ghost theory probably never heard, or discarded if they did. For instance, a half-educated—and, according to some, half-cracked—Mexican called *"El Santo"* insisted that *chisos* was derived from the plural of *chis*—a word I never heard before or since, but according to him it meant the clash of arms in battle— and that at night you could hear the clash of steel on steel as the ghosts of Spanish warriors killed in battles with the Indians came out to fight their battles over again.

Almost at the beginning of my inquiries, an intelligent, self-educated Mexican told me he had heard that the mountains got their name from a tribe of Indians, called in their own monosyllabic language *Chis-sah.* A good many years later old Tom Burnham, who hauled freight for the soldiers at old Fort Davis and listened to the stories of the Mexicans as early as the 1870's, told me that he had also heard that the mountains were named for a tribe of Indians.

In the 1930's I got some surprising confirmation of

this. The late Mr. E. E. Townsend, sometimes called
the father of the Big Bend Park, dug up some old records in Spanish that told the story of this tribe which
the Spaniards called *Chizo*. This tribe had such hor-
rible customs, including cannibalism, that the other
Indians joined the Spaniards in wiping them entirely
out of existence. There seems no doubt that Indians of
this name once existed. Whether the mountains really
got their name from them is, of course, something else
again.

Then there is the theory that *chisos* is a corruption of
hechizos, a Spanish word of many meanings mostly
dealing with witchcraft, charms, spells, and black
magic. *Hechizos* is pronounced with the *h* silent, short
e, *i* like *ee*, *z* like *s*—"Eh-chee-sos"—and sounds very
much like *chisos*.

One meaning of the word *hechizo* is, according to my
all Spanish dictionary, "that which charms or enchants
by beauty or good qualities." Some well-educated and
informed Mexicans believe that this is the real meaning of the name, that is, "Mountain of Charms" or
"Enchantments." Possibly they are right. Maybe some
old explorer, struck by the wonderful scenery, gave
them this beautiful name.

On the other hand, the word *hechizo* is most com-
monly used in the sense of witchcraft or powers derived from evil forces. In no case does it mean "ghost,"

but since in all cases it deals with the supernatural it is easy to see that both the word and the meaning might have gotten slightly twisted into *chisos*—meaning "ghosts."

There is an interesting story that ties in with this, insofar as any old legend may be accepted as evidence —a story of hidden treasure and black magic.

It says that when this country still belonged to Spain, a party of men were forced to leave the Chisos Mountains and leave behind a large amount of gold. The details are not clear as to whether these men had stolen the gold and were in hiding or whether this is connected with the more famous story of the Lost Chisos Mine. It seems more clear that they had to leave because of danger from the Indians.

At any rate, they hid the money in a cave. Now one of these men was a *brujo* or *hechicero*, that is, a wizard, who could cast spells or charms, and before they left the cave he made his incantations and cast a spell that no one could break but him. Invoking the Powers of Darkness, he fixed it so that no one could take the gold away until he returned.

On the way out, the party was almost entirely wiped out by Indians. The *hechicero*, whose charms didn't seem to work against Indian arrows, was among those killed.

The survivors told the story, and later some of them

returned. Others also tried to carry the gold away but the magic of the dead wizard still held. Some managed to enter the cave, but none could pick up the gold. Thus the mountain came to be called *Cerro del Hechizo*, which in time was shortened to *Chizo* and later applied to the whole mountain range and called Chisos.

The story persists to this day. One old Mexican told me, with a perfectly straight face, that once while hunting deer he found the cave with its stacks of gold bars, but when he stooped to pick one up he became almost paralyzed and couldn't straighten up. In terror, he managed to creep out of the cave, and he never went back. Another old Mexican, now so feeble he can hardly walk, assures me that, with a rosary and cross and certain words of prayer that only he knows, he can overcome the Powers of Darkness and carry away the treasure, bewitched or not.

Might be a good idea to get these two men together—one to guide you to the cave, and the other to carry out the gold. Any takers?

At any rate, all this is what I have heard about the origin of the word *chisos* during many years of trying to get the facts. Facts or not—that's "the way I heard it."

The Chisos Mine

The story of the mining industry in the Big Bend is too big and too complicated to tell in a single chapter. Though it merits at least one volume, I will tell briefly the story of the principal mercury producer at Terlingua, most of these items also being "the way I heard it."

At the beginning, Terlingua seems to have been an Indian village at the place where the creek, also called Terlingua, flows into the Río Grande. I say "seems to be," because this part is mostly hearsay and legend.

It has often been stated that the word *terlingua* is a corruption of the Spanish words *tres lenguas,* meaning "three tongues." To a person who has studied this matter as much as I have, this theory seems far-fetched and unlikely. It seems more likely that it was an original Indian word whose meaning has been long lost.

At any rate, there are stories which indicate that there were Spanish-speaking people there as early as about 1800. There were certainly Mexican settlers in the vicinity in 1859 when a troop of the U.S. Cavalry arrived there with pack mules and pack camels. Probably the Mexicans were forced out several times by raiding Indians, but always came back.

When the Indians were finally disposed of in about 1880, Terlingua became a prosperous farming and ranching community, though it was one hundred miles from a railroad. Quicksilver was discovered and mines were opened, a brick factory was established, a church built, a school and a post office were opened. About that time the Mariposa Mine was booming, and the post office was moved there, about fifteen miles from the original site. This new place was for a time called Terlingua, while the original place was usually called *Terlingua Vieja* or *Terlingua Baja*.

Back about the end of the past century and the beginning of the present, when there was already some mercury being mined in modest quantity in the region, two men named McKinney and Parker[6] were camped near the present site of the Chisos Mine, now abandoned. There was a third man, but he seems, in time, to have disappeared, while Parker and McKinney both lived to a good old age and died in the Big Bend. Both died as befitted old timers, "with their boots on," active to the last.

The story says that they were hunting "mavericks" —wild, unbranded cattle—and were only casually prospecting for minerals. If that was so, they casually

[6] Devine McKinney and Jess Parker, whose claims in 1900 and 1901 joined the Chisos Mine property on the west. McKinney and Parker formed the Rainbow Mining Company, which they lost in a mortgage foreclosure by the Terlingua Mining Company in 1904.

and accidentally stumbled onto a fortune, but, as it turned out, for another man.

At any rate, they found a rich deposit of cinnabar, the bright red rock from which mercury is produced. The country had been only recently surveyed and, on investigation, they found that the land on which this discovery was located belonged to a man named Howard E. Perry, who was in the lumber business in Portland, Maine. They first wired and later wrote Perry in an attempt to buy the land. Becoming suspicious, Perry wrote to a lawyer in Alpine named Van Sickle,[7] to investigate. Acting on Van Sickle's report, Perry began mining operations on the spot, forming what he called "The Chisos Mining Company." Since he was the sole owner, though, it was not a company, and the land was some thirty miles from the mountains called Chisos.

Meanwhile, Parker and McKinney filed a mining claim on a state section joining Perry's section on the south and only a short distance from Perry's workings. They secured financial backing and sunk a shaft. It may be assumed that they were not expert miners, as the venture was not profitable, and they finally sold out to Perry, who worked it to more advantage and realized a fair profit.

McKinney and Parker both died poor men. Mc-

[7] Judge Wigfall Van Sickle (1863–1941).

Kinney died of a heart attack on a prospecting trip in the Christmas Mountains a few miles northeast of Terlingua. Although an old man, he was still trying like a true disciple of Coronado to make the earth give up its treasures. Some years previously, Parker had been found dead by his horse on a mountain trail near Boquillas, Texas, and is still buried at the spot where he was found.

Perry's mine ran the first few years at a loss, but soon developed into the largest producer in the region. No figures are available, but profits must have been well into the millions. I have been told by a man who was employed in the smelter at the time that, during the First World War, when mercury was selling at an all-time high, the mine was clearing, net, more than two thousand dollars per day.[8]

A farm properly farmed lasts forever; a pasture if not overgrazed will continue sustaining animals indefinitely; and a forest handled scientifically will keep on producing lumber or pulpwood as long as the rain falls and the seasons come and go. But what is taken from a mine is gone forever, as far as that mine is concerned.

[8] In its peak year of 1917, the Terlingua area produced 10,791 flasks, valued at $1,136,508. In 1922, Howard Perry's Chisos Mine supplied 40 per cent of the quicksilver produced in the United States that year.—Madison, *The Big Bend Country*, pp. 187, 188.

A mine has no way of replenishing itself, and no matter how high the owner's profits go, sooner or later he must face a loss.

So the so-called Chisos Mine, after more than forty years as the hub of the mining industry in that region, began to play out. Perry, then around ninety, seems to have lost his grip. The mine was sold at sheriff's sale, and in 1941, Howard Perry died. The new owners tried to work it for a few years, but were finally forced to close down at considerable loss. The great Chisos Mine was through.

For more than thirty years the Chisos Mining Company's town, while it was known as Terlingua, was the center of business and social life of the region as well as the mining industry. It employed from one hundred to three hundred men, and the camp had a population of five hundred to a thousand. The general store sold not only to the miners but to the ranchers and smaller mines. There were a church and a five-room schoolhouse in the town, a hotel and cafe, and at one time a picture show. There were baseball and basketball teams that gave neighboring towns some stiff competition. Company C, Infantry, Texas State Guard, was at one time made up entirely of Terlingua boys.

When the name "Terlingua"—which had been moved from the little farming community called Terlingua to the Mariposa Mine—was moved again to the

Chisos Mine and that place took the name of "Terlingua," the Mexican people never accepted the
change. To them Terlingua still meant the village at
the mouth of the creek of that name, and they still to
this day call the mining village "Chisos."

Today Terlingua, or Chisos, is a ghost town. In 1946
it closed down for good. Houses and machinery were
torn down and moved away, and today it is a ghost
town where the ruins look like they have been atom-
bombed. Most of the buildings have been torn down,
and those left standing look rather sad to us who still
remember the booming mining camp. Even the post
office has moved over on Terlingua Creek where water
is more readily available, for when the mine pumps
stopped for the last time, there was no more water.
Only two Mexican families live there now. The post
office and school (which has only nine pupils) have
moved to another site six miles east on Terlingua
Creek.

Thus Terlingua has "moved" three times—from
farming and ranching village to booming mining
camp, to another booming mining camp, and at last
back to the corn and the beans and the goats and the
cows.

4. Will James: Big Bend Superman

In every land, and in every line of endeavor, there are men who stand above and beyond their fellows in brains, physical strength, courage, pure cussedness, or in a dozen other ways. Influenced by heredity or environment, men are *not* equal. In any frontier land the two things that stand out most are courage and physical prowess. And the saga of the Big Bend is rich with the stories of men in whom these were developed to the highest level.

The great-great-great grandpappy of them all was Alvar Núñez, called Cabeza de Vaca, or "Cowshead," who more than four hundred years ago walked barefooted, unarmed, and practically naked across Texas and the Big Bend when the country was a howling wilderness, than which there ain't been no howlinger. (Yes, I know. Some historians claim he never was in the Big Bend, but that's the story, and besides this isn't history.) It is not related that his was a great physical strength, but his endurance, fortitude, and never-say-die courage stood at an all time high.

After him came others, most of whom flourished and sank without a trace in that vast ocean of illiteracy which covered this part of the earth at the time. Only fragments of the stories remain of such legendary heroes as El Cíbolo, El Piocho, the Spanish Creole Santiago, Bajo Sol, the Indian Santiago Alsate, and others. I have already told something from the scant and obscure tales of some of these men, and the rest of this chapter will be about a man of our own time and the stories told to me by men who knew him.

His name was Will James, and he lived in the Big Bend in the late 1800's and early 1900's. Easterners would have called him a cowboy. He was, in fact, a ranchman, in a small way—maverick hunter, mostly, and some unkind neighbors called him a cow thief. He had a way of starting out with a horse and saddle, a pair of rawhide hobbles, a long rope and a branding iron, a slicker for a bed, and a *morral* (feed bag) for a trunk and commissary. By buying a cow here and there, catching more mavericks than anybody, and making each cow raise from two to a half-dozen calves each season, he soon built up a good-sized little herd. Then he would sell everything, go to El Paso or some other city and stay. When his money was all blown in, he would go back to the Big Bend, borrow a horse and saddle, sometimes without even asking the owner, and start all over again.

So far, there is nothing remarkable about him. The qualities which made him stand out were physical courage, unbelievable strength, and coordination, so that I would not believe the stories of his remarkable feats, except that I knew the men who told them were not given to exaggeration. It is told that he could stand flat-footed and jump over a saddled horse. He was so fleet of foot that he could overtake and pull down a wild cow on the open prairie. He was so skillful with a rope that he could lasso coyotes and jack rabbits and he was, of course, a marvelous horseman. He could exist for days or weeks on no more bed or food than he could carry hung on his saddle, and could find his way over the roughest country in the dark and brand a few mavericks on the way.

On the range he was something of a lone wolf. In town, in a crowd, he was just the opposite: a bounding extravert, a show-off, and a clown. And I have never heard of his having a fight or any trouble with anybody. Maybe his marvelous strength and skill, which he was always showing off, discouraged those who might have been inclined to resent his clowning capers.

Sometimes, when he saw a man on the street wearing a derby hat or some other mark of the effete East, he would circle around the stranger, tossing his head and pawing and snorting like a mustang. Once when he entered a cafe, dirty and ragged with several months' growth of beard on his face, he spied a drummer just preparing to eat a large juicy steak. With his big knife Will James speared the steak, dragged it over to his side of the table, and proceeded to devour it with all the exquisite table manners of a lobo wolf, growling and snarling, while the drummer looked glumly on.

In the country, too, when he had an audience he never failed to come through with some startling and unusual stunt. Once when a man and his wife drove up in a buggy to James' camp, he was just returning from hobbling his horse and was carrying a rope in his hand. He had left a pair of freshly tallowed rawhide hobbles in his camp, and a coyote was gnawing away on them. Whirling a loop and making a sudden dash, he lassoed the coyote on the run. Hauling the scared beast in, he proceeded to whale the daylights out of the coyote, all the while cussing him for a thief. Finally, admonishing Mr. Coyote never to be guilty of such again, he slipped off the rope and administered a final kick. Then he turned, with great surprise, to greet his visitors though he no doubt knew they were there all the time.

He seemed to have an unerring instinct about animals, both wild and domestic, and always seemed to know what they would or would not do. Once when he and some other fellows were chasing a large panther with a pack of dogs, the panther took refuge in a cave on a mountainside. Will James wanted to see the dogs chase the panther some more, so he went back in the cave and booted the panther out. To this day, this place is called Panther Mountain.[1]

His most noted stunt was winning a foot race. Not because he won—that was to be expected. It was the way he did it. It seems there was a July Fourth barbecue and along came a traveling athlete, very common in those days. A city slicker usually carried one or more of these athletes—foot racers, boxers, or wrestlers—around rural areas, took on the local yokels, and usually won. On this occasion it was a foot racer and his manager, so the local citizens at once offered to match Will James against him for any amount of money.

Will had just come in off the range, and as usual was dirty, ragged, and unshaven. He wore a pair of old

[1] Panther Mountain is in sight of the Park Ranger Station at Panther Junction, at the entrance on Texas State Highway 227 to the Big Bend National Park.

broken and run-down boots, with huge Mexican spurs. He looked like anything but a foot racer, while the professional was slim and trim and was wearing racing trunks and spiked shoes. At the sight of him, James began to circle around, pawing and snorting. He pulled off his disreputable boots and threw them as far as he could in opposite directions. As the men lined up to start, the professional went into the starting crouch, but James stood upright, prancing and pawing the earth with his bare feet.

They broke away even and ran along evenly enough for a way. Then suddenly with a wild yell James dashed past the stranger, ran a complete circle around him, and ran on to win the race, still looking back like a wild mule and snorting like a mustang, while the crowd went wild.

What became of Will James? Well, nobody, not even a superman, lasts forever. The years passed and Will was no longer young. The great open range was being fenced and mavericks were getting scarcer. The G–4 ranch, the biggest source of mavericks, closed out and left the country. It was a sad day for the mavericks when the last G–4 bovine left the Big Bend.

Will worked for a while in a smelter of one of the quicksilver mines in south Brewster County. This monotonous and confining job must have galled his free-ranging soul, for he soon gave it up and drifted farther west. Years later, word came back of his death.

A certain poetic gent once compared the years to great, black oxen marching slowly and inexorably onward. Fleet-footed Will James could overtake and tail down a wild cow on the open prairie, but he couldn't escape those slow-plodding, black oxen. They finally overtook him.

5. Outlaws and *Bandidos*

The Ketchum Train Robbery

This story starts on one day, I think, in 1912. I rode into Sheffield, Texas, riding one horse and leading another with a light pack. I tied my horses in front of the general store and went in to inquire about work. Ten minutes later I had a job with a man named Martin, who had a ranch about six miles south of town.

Martin had about fifteen hundred Angora goats, about one hundred head of stock horses, and no cattle. As there was no house on the ranch, Martin and his wife and three children lived in Sheffield. A Mexican goat-herder and I camped out on the ranch. My job was to hunt lost goats, if any, to look after horses, fences, and windmills, to see that the herder was kept in grub and water, and to keep an eye on things generally.

Sheffield at that time had a reputation as a pretty tough place. In fact, law enforcement was rather lax. Situated near the borders of Pecos, Crockett, and Terrell counties, it was approximately seventy-five, forty, and sixty miles, respectively, from the three county seats, and remember, this was still in the horse and buggy days, cars not yet having come into general use. Often there was no representative of the law present for months at a time. Other than this, however, I think it was the background of some of its citizens that gave the place its reputation. Individuals who had killed their man (or men) were common, and others were blood relatives of some of the most noted outlaws in the Southwest.

There was old Berry Ketchum, brother to Tom Ketchum ("Black Jack") who was hanged in 1901 for murder, robbery, and outlawry. Another Ketchum, named Sam, was killed while trying to rob a train. Old Berry, who, as far as is known, never took part in any of these robberies, ranched near Sheffield. Then there was Boone Kilpatrick[1] and his younger brother Felix, who were not known to have ever taken part in any outlawry but they were full brothers to two noted out-

[1] Boone Kilpatrick died in December, 1958, at Iraan, Texas, having served there as Constable for many years.

laws—bank and train robbers. One brother, whose name was George, had disappeared without a trace. It was generally believed that he had died probably from gunshot wounds and had been buried in some remote hide-out, or else, seeing the handwriting on the wall, had taken his share of the loot and left for parts unknown. The other brother was Ben, also called "Blackie," and, as a member of the Hole-in-the-Wall Gang, sometimes called "The Tall Texan." He had been caught with the goods and sent to the penitentiary about ten years before the time of this story.

Mrs. Martin briefed me on all these people's background. She had an idea that I was a nice boy who should still be with his mother and should only associate with Sunday-school characters. This amused me very much, as I had been mostly on my own since I was fourteen, and had seen gun fights and had known some pretty hard *hombres*. Among the most noted of these was Henry Ransome, whom I had known and worked with on a ranch. As a peace officer, ranger, and soldier-scout in the Philippines, and just for the hell of it as a private individual, he was said to have killed thirty men. So I was neither scared nor thrilled by fearsome reputations.

That summer, Ben Kilpatrick was released from the pen, his term shortened by good behavior and other devices, and he came to Sheffield. For a short time, being very friendly with Boone and Felix, I saw him frequently.

I had to look up to Ben from my gangling, youthful, six-foot-one. Boone and Felix were tall men—blondish and inclined to corpulency—but Ben was taller than either of them. He carried no surplus fat. He was dark and had dark piercing eyes that looked through and beyond you. Boone and Felix laughed easily. I never saw Ben smile. Though just out of prison, he wore expensive clothes and a Stetson hat that would have set me back a month's wages at that time. He was handsome in a dark, sinister way, and I think he could have made more money in the movies than by robbing trains. The way things turned out, I'm sure of it.

He was around Sheffield off and on for several months. He appeared and disappeared with suspicious abruptness. During that time there were several minor bank robberies. Some of the people suspected Ben, though at the time I thought little of it one way or the other.

Boone had a small ranch which lay between Martin's ranch and Sheffield. Felix lived in "town" and sometimes worked on ranches. His wife ran the telephone "central." More than thirty years later, I was surprised to read in a newspaper article that Sheffield had never had a telephone exchange. There was certainly one there in the year 1911–12.

My boss, Martin, was away a good deal, shipping
horses to Louisiana and Arkansas. About February or
March, I was getting ready for spring goat-shearing.
The goat-herder, a Mexican named Elario Rodríguez,
was twenty-three or twenty-four years old, only a few
years older than I. He was six feet tall, intelligent, and
strong as a bull. Although working as a common herder
at the time, he usually had a better job. As he was
honest and capable, ranchmen would leave him in
charge of thousands of dollars worth of livestock for
weeks, or even months, at a time. I have never seen his
equal for tracking or reading signs, and I have seen
few men of any race that I liked and trusted more.

I was readying the shearing pens and building
shades to protect the freshly shorn animals, when I
decided to go to town to see if I could learn when the
shearing crew would arrive. On the way I passed Kilpatrick's ranch house. I could see three men on the
front porch, apparently playing cards. When they saw
me, two of them scuttled inside on all fours. One
straightened up in the entrance, and his head almost
touched the top of the doorway—Ben, without a doubt.

The third man was Felix, though he was supposed to
be working on the lower John Cannon Ranch at the
time. He met me at the front gate, talked, hoorawed,
and told stories, but did not invite me in.

I am usually good at minding my own business, so I

rode on and told nobody what I had seen. But a few days later a man named Hub Stone, who was building some fence nearby, told me of seeing a man in Boone's back yard who immediately ducked and hustled into the house.

"Maybe it was Ben," I said. "Was it a tall man with a white Stetson?"

"No," Hub said. "He was a skinny, hatchet-faced feller and he wore a cap."

A few days later we learned what day the shearing crew would arrive. Elario brought the goats in and put them in a small pasture. The next day he went back to see if any stragglers had been left on the larger range. He came back looking very serious.

"*Oiga tu,*" he said. "Listen! I saw something I don't understand, but I think it is not good."

He went on to say that some horsemen had passed along the road the night before, heading south. Nothing strange about that, but on the road the horsemen had met two vehicles and both times had turned out to avoid being seen by the drivers. At one place where the riders had stopped, Elario found a brand new cartridge. It was a .380 automatic pistol cartridge, the first I had ever seen. Then I went with him to look at the tracks, and it was just as he said.

"Who do you think they are?" I asked.

"*Yo creo los* Ketchies." He meant Ketchums. I must

have looked incredulous, for he went on: "Not *El Viejo* Ketchie. He is an old man, but he keeps young men around him. Look at these tracks. They are not the cup-shaped hoofs of common cow ponies, nor of *patones*, those awkward ducks like Mr. Martin our *patrón* raises. These horses are *de cría ligero* (racing stock). Only the Ketchum Ranch has horses like that." As it turned out, he was only partly right. They were Ketchum horses, but they did not carry Ketchum riders.

A few days later we were busy with the shearing crew, when Hub Stone came by to tell us the news. Two men had been killed trying to rob a Southern Pacific train between Dryden and Sanderson, Texas, which lay directly south.

Shortly afterward, Felix Kilpatrick came by, as he often did, on his way from Cannon's ranch to Sheffield. Usually he stopped to kid with us and drink coffee or eat a lunch. This time he looked neither right nor left, but urged his horse, a fast-pacing bay, on past us with frantic haste. Instantly all was clear. I no longer wondered if the two men hiding at Kilpatrick's ranch were the robbers. I knew!

The story of the attempted robbery goes something like this:

About dark one evening the westbound local Southern Pacific passenger train pulled into Dryden. It usually pauses or stops there for only a moment. This time, as the wheels began to roll, some boys standing nearby saw a man slip out of the shadows and trot toward the locomotive. He was a giant of a man, wearing overalls and a jumper. A cap, pulled low, and a dark handkerchief hid his face. As the train gathered speed, he swung on board the engine and the train disappeared into the night.

Once on board, the intruder produced an automatic pistol and gave the engine crew their instructions, adding, "Do as I tell you and you won't be hurt."

About halfway between Dryden and Sanderson, in an almost uninhabited region, a long bridge crosses a deep canyon. It was of the type known as an "open deck"—just ties bolted to a framework of stringers. When the engineer, threatened by the stranger's pistol, brought the train to a stop on this bridge, nobody could get off without risking a fall to the bottom of the canyon. The train crew and passengers were cut off from the front of the train.

As the engine ground to a halt, a smaller, slimmer man, dressed and masked like the big man, climbed on board. "All right, Frank," he said, "I'll take the hogger." Throughout, he addressed the big man as Frank.

The big man went back and uncoupled the express car, or maybe had one of the engine crew do it, and the engine inched it forward a short way. Also, by threats or some means they got the express car door open, and the big man began systematically looting the car. It has been said that there was a large amount of money on board and that the bandits must have had inside information.

There are differing versions of what followed. One story says that the express messenger pulled the old trick of suddenly looking and pointing behind the robber. Another says that he indicated a package on the floor and told the robber that it was the most valuable package in the car, and the big man stooped to pick it up.

At any rate, the robber was caught off guard, and the messenger smashed the big man's head with a wooden mallet and, as he fell, struck him again and again.

The messenger picked up the fallen automatic and fired a shot in the air, then waited. Soon he could hear the other bandit calling, "Frank! Frank! What's the matter?"

Getting no answer, the bandit cautiously stuck his head around the door facing, only to get a bullet through his brain. End of train robbery.

The two corpses were taken into Sanderson, where the tall man was quickly identified as Ben Kilpatrick. The other man was Ed Welsh, called "Old Beck" by his pals. It was believed that he had been in prison with

Ben. He was about fifty—skinny, stooped, and as Hub Stone said, "hatchet-faced."[2]

Two saddled horses were found at the scene of the holdup. Elario had been right, for they wore the K brand of the Ketchum Ranch. Old Berry Ketchum indignantly denied any knowledge of how they came into the robbers' possession. It was easy to believe him, as the Ketchums and the Kilpatricks were bitter enemies.

Although that last pistol shot put a quietus on the train robbery, as well as on the two robbers, one question remains. That is, who were their accomplices?

Eavesdroppers said that when Felix's wife phoned him at Cannon's ranch, she told him that "two of them are killed already." How did they know that the express car would be carrying a large sum of money? Who stole the Ketchum horses? Not they. They knew neither the country nor the horses. Who spotted that particular bridge and knew it would tie up crew and passengers in their cars? Maybe "Hatchet-Face" had been a railroad man. Notice that he called the engineer a "hogger." And finally, how did Ben get to Dryden from where his horse was, many miles away?

There is a story of a mysterious stranger with a buggy and team, who appeared in Dryden that night

[2] See also Ed Bartholomew, *Black Jack Ketchum: Last of the Hold-up Kings,* The Frontier Press of Texas, Houston, 1955, pp. 104–105.

and disappeared, just as mysteriously, before dawn. It is even told that the buggy and team were found but the man was never seen again. If there was a third horseman at the scene of the holdup, he doubtless put many miles behind him before dawn.

Quoting from a well-known poem, "Hardly a man is now alive who remembers that famous day and year," and knows enough to fill in all the missing details. Felix Kilpatrick was shot and killed shortly afterward by his erstwhile bosom companion, and my friend Elario was stabbed to death during a drunken free-for-all in a house of ill fame.

Es la vida—y la muerte. That's life—and death.

Río Grande Justice

For many many years there have appeared, in various publications, stories or articles about Mexican *bandidos*, mostly written by men who couldn't even pronounce the word correctly and who certainly knew nothing of the bandits themselves. And goodness knows where they got all the ideas they put into print, as we who live on the border could never recognize our neighbors by the descriptions given of them.

In the May of 1933 a Big Bend rancher named Art

Hannold crossed the Río Grande to look for some strayed animals. He was captured and held for several days by some Mexicans. Their leader was named Candelario Baiza. The newspapers played this Baiza up as a bandit chieftain and Hannold as a cattle baron of the Big Bend. Now most of us know that Baiza was a rather stupid and ignorant fellow who was dangerous largely because of his ignorance and stupidity, while Art, like most of us who live here, was just a poor boy trying to get by, raising a few cattle in a desert.

Besides the Baizas, there were other families whose sons played bandit along the border for a number of years. Some of these were the Jordan brothers. Their ancestor was an Irishman, and one story says he was a soldier of fortune who came into Mexico with Maximilian as a member of the French Foreign Legion, and remained in Mexico after the French troops were withdrawn. Now there is no *j* sound in Spanish, so Jordan's descendants changed the pronunciation rather than the spelling of their name. The *j* is sounded like *h* and the *d* softened until it sounds almost like *th*—"Hor-than."

The heyday of the Jordans was during the Mexican Revolution. One of them was said to have cut the throats of a dozen men of the opposite faction while they were all tied hand and foot. Because of this and other acts, the Jordans were unpopular, so when a measure of law and order came to northern Mexico they left the country, and none of them live opposite the Big Bend at present.

This chapter, however, is largely the story of the Domínguez clan. They were all born within a few miles of the Río Grande on the Texas side of the border at a ranch which most of us still call the Domínguez Place.

Although I do not know their complete family tree, there is no doubt that they had a large percentage of the blood of the old wild Indians who once ranged those same hills and mountains. They were light, slender men, slightly below medium height, with the sharp, rather aquiline features usually associated with fighting Indians. They were unexcelled as horsemen, mountaineers, and woodsmen, and, though I believe they feared nothing on earth, they had a canny caution and took few unnecessary chances.

They were not the sort of bad men who killed their enemies in public and afterwards paraded the notches on their guns. If it became necessary for them to kill a man, the offending citizen usually just disappeared, with little or nothing to connect his disappearance with the Domínguez boys. Although they gave a good account of themselves in all the gun battles and forays in which they took part, this was not their game. And I doubt if even down to the end of their career they could have been convicted in court, so skillfully and smoothly did they operate at all times. They early showed signs of outlawry. Although all of them were very young at the time, it was believed that they guided the Villista forces in the Glenn Springs raid in 1916. An older Domínguez was killed in a gun battle with the Rangers about 1920.

Of the remaining brothers, the ones who gave the officers the worst headaches were Patricio (called Picho), Marceliono, and Juan. Being Texas-born, they operated freely on both sides of the river, and often worked on Texas ranches. They were top cowhands and star bronc-busters and ropers. Also, they were by no means unpleasant fellows, being full of wit and humor, although their humor was sometimes pretty crude.

They were callously indifferent to the sufferings of either man or beast, and would ride a horse until he dropped, just for fun. They tell that once when Picho returned from one of his nefarious expeditions he rode up to his house and stripped the saddle and bridle off his horse, which at once laid down, or rather, fell down, in the doorway.

"Válgame Dios, hijo!" said his mother. "Bless my soul, son! Shame on you. Just look at that poor, tired animal!"

"If he's tired, what do you think I am?" asked Picho. "I've ridden him a hundred miles."

Since their technique was always to get at least one

more jump out of a horse before it dropped dead, they could always do more on a horse than anybody else, even though the horse died immediately after, or was never any good any more. They could always steal another.

Once when some officers were on the trail of Juan and some more Mexicans who had stolen a bunch of horses, they saw where one of the riders had left the rest and started in pursuit of a deer. The trail of deer and horse disappeared into the hills, but presently the officers crossed it again. Out of curiosity they followed the trail a way and found where the rider had ridden up by the side of the tiring deer and killed it with a knife. He did not shoot the deer, as there was no bullet hole in the hide. He did not lasso it, as there were no signs of a struggle such as even a tired deer would have made if caught with a rope. He simply ran by the side of the deer and slashed its side with a knife. The deer ran on a few yards, spilling blood and trailing entrails, and then dropped dead. In a rough and broken country, on an unshod horse, Juan had already been riding for days on nothing but grass, and he had ridden down and killed with a knife a black-tailed deer, one of the fleetest and cagiest animals in these mountains.

Under different circumstances the Domínguez boys might have been bank or train robbers. They might have been minor leaders in a revolution. As it was, they were smugglers, horse thieves, and smalltime bandits. They all came to maturity during the Prohibition era, and their game was mostly running contraband liquor. Nobody much objected to this, as I believe that most of the citizens of the Big Bend, being freedom-loving and hardy individualists, were lukewarm, to say the least, about Mr. Volstead's noble experiment. But when the smugglers stole horses, butchered calves, and took to shooting at officers, that was something else again. Although nobody had a great love for the Volstead minions and rather enjoyed seeing the smugglers make monkeys out of them, nobody wanted to see them get killed—not by any such breed of coyotes as the Domínguez boys, anyhow.

Down here they didn't believe in turning over to the law a man who had otherwise been a good citizen just because he brought a jug of liquor across the border or added to his herd a calf or colt from Mexico. So when small-scale smuggling was reported to the federal officers you could be pretty sure that it was because the smuggler was doing something unneighborly like stealing or taking a pot shot at somebody from ambush.

Some of these liquor-runners were very careful about observing the rules. Others, including the Domínguez boys, were not. Since they were the hardest men in the country on their horses, they were always short of saddle and pack animals, and would pick

these up wherever they needed them and turn loose
their tired, footsore and sore-backed animals anytime
they could steal fresh ones. Since their pack animals
were always loaded down with liquor, the smugglers
never carried much food, but they butchered ranchmen's calves indiscriminately along the route. More
than once they fired on officers or men they thought
might be officers when they got too close.

These activities made the Domínguez boys' operations unpopular. Although they were never caught at
any of these things, most ranchmen in this country can
read tracks and signs like a city man reads a newspaper, and nobody was fooled about who was doing
all this. So the Domínguez boys and their friends became more and more unwelcome, and had to seek
newer routes and dimmer trails, continually.

It was, I think, about '33 or '34 when some cowmen,
of which I was one, were gathering cattle in the foot-
hills of the Solitarios northwest of Terlingua. We saw
Marcelo Domínguez, with his pack mules loaded with
liquor, headed in the direction of Alpine. With him
was a slim dudish-looking Mexican who was wearing
army officer boots and who spoke good English. None
of us knew him, but we all knew Marcelo. We shook
hands, took a drink together, and they went on their
way and we went on about our business.

They reached Alpine, safely disposed of their load,

and started back. Now a ranch near Alpine had lost some saddle horses, and the ranchers were sure these men had gotten them on a previous trip, so they reported to the officers the route the smugglers had taken coming in, and which they might be expected to take going back, and also when they might be expected to arrive at a certain place.

There were both federal and county officers waiting for the Mexicans at this place. When ordered to surrender, the smugglers opened fire, and the officers began shooting back. Marcelo was killed by the first volley. A high-powered rifle bullet struck him in the neck and he probably never knew his career was ending. The other Mexican abandoned horses and pack mules, took to the brush afoot, and miraculously got away through a hail of bullets. Two days later he showed up at a ranch near the border some sixty or seventy miles away and asked for something to eat.

The Prohibition era was ending about this time, and the day of the liquor-runners was about over. But many of them didn't seem to realize it, and kept on trying to sell liquor, though the price of illegal booze was away down.

Although the officers in Texas were on the lookout for Picho Domínguez, the officers in Mexico got so hot on his trail that he had to dodge across into Texas, where he established himself in a hide-out as a sort of middleman handling smuggled liquor. Some seven or eight miles west of Terlingua near the old Mariposa Mine is a round-topped mountain called on the map "Black Mesa," though it is neither a mesa nor black. Local Americans call it Round Mountain, while Mexicans call it *Cerro de la Matanza, matanza* meaning slaughter, or massacre, a wholesale killing. *Cerro* means a lone mountain—Slaughter Mountain.

How it got this bloodcurdling name is a very prosaic story. In the early 1900's when the Mariposa Mine was booming, a Mexican ran a meat market there and sold mostly goat meat. He kept a flock of goats on this mountain, at the foot of which he had a slaughter pen where he butchered several goats each day for his market. The name still sticks.

It was on this mountain that Picho and another Mexican named Prejádes Galindo established themselves. A local Mexican who had a wagon and some burros was camped nearby. They would cut grass on this mountain, tie it in bundles, and haul it into Terlingua or other camps to sell for hay. Under this hay would be concealed whatever liquor they thought they could sell that trip. A local man did the selling. Picho, being wanted on both sides of the border, laid pretty low. However, a great many people knew he was there, and if he had behaved himself nobody would have bothered him. He could not let well enough alone, however. He was soon up to his old tricks, butchering other people's cattle and stealing their horses, so the ranchmen told the officers what was going on.

The officers raided the smugglers' camp one morning about dawn. There were a U.S. Customs officer, a Ranger, and some local officers. Each of these men has explained to me why the raid was bungled so that it was only partly successful. My own opinion is that it was because they were made up of so many different branches of the law without recognized head or authority, for all these men were good officers. The two outlaws got away after an exchange of shots. The officers captured their camp, bedding, saddles, pack saddles, and equipment, out of which they made a bonfire. They also captured a number of stolen horses.

Since then Picho has stuck pretty close to the south side of the Río Grande. The last news I had of him was that he had about made his peace with the Mexican officers and was going to marry a widow with some property.

About 1930 Juan Domínguez was mixed up in the killing of two men on the Texas side, and for some nine or ten years thereafter he came back to Texas only to steal and rob and terrorize humble and harmless people of his own race. It was on one of these forays, while the officers were following him, that the deer-killing episode took place. On this occasion the American officers, accompanied by three Mexican officers, followed Juan and his gang some fifty miles into Mexico, but never caught up with him.

There is in Mexico an organization, a kind of brotherhood with police powers, called *La Acordada*, but local people say *'Cordada*. It means "The Court," but it is something of a combination of the Texas Rangers and the vigilance committees of the Old West, with a Mexican flavor, if you can imagine that.

The captain of the *'Cordada* just across the border from here, a man named Corona, is a man of resolution, and is plenty hard-boiled when necessary. His men are all local men who can ride and shoot almost as well as any Domínguez. This *'Cordada* finally decided to put an end to Juan's nefarious activities, so they proceeded to his village and surrounded the house where he and his friends had barricaded themselves.

"Either come out and surrender or send your women and children out. In ten minutes we start shooting!" ordered Corona.

So Juan and his pals came out and surrendered. They were taken as prisoners to San Carlos. After a few days they were released, mostly because the Domínguez boys, due to their smooth work and terrorizing of witnesses, could never be convicted in court.

Corona gave them a final talk. He told them he knew they had a hard time making a living in that barren country, but that they must stop killing and stealing. He asked them to call on him for financial aid, rather than turn to crime again.

"But," he added, "if you do go on like you have been, you will surely face a firing squad."

So Juan and his pals returned to their old haunts. Far from being good, they were if anything worse than ever. They had been in the toils of the law, and the law hadn't done anything with them. Besides, they had to take revenge on those people who, so they believed, had reported them to the *'Cordada.*

So a good time was had by all but the victims, until suddenly Corona and his men appeared again. They took Juan and one Lorenzo Hinojos, chained in the back seat of a car, to San Carlos. Juan spoke to a member of the *'Cordada* who drove the car.

"Tell me, *compadre,*" he said, although they were not compadres, "are they going to finish me?"

The driver replied, "There is no remedy now, *compadre.* Your time has come."

The two men were taken from the car at San Carlos and tied onto horses. A man who lives in San Carlos said he heard Corona order one of his men to take a shovel.

"What for?" asked the man.

"I'll make the so-and-so's dig their own grave," said Corona.

The men were taken, tied on their horses, some twelve miles north to the Río Grande in the almost un-inhabited country opposite Lajitas, Texas. Corona sent over to the store on the Texas side and bought some coffee for his men. A Mexican who lived at Lajitas crossed over to see the prisoners. He was allowed to greet but not converse with them. Corona kept them seated at a fire with a man guarding them from a distance with a rifle, and not even his own men were allowed to approach or converse with them. As the time of their execution arrived, Lorenzo Hinojos went to pieces, shaking and blubbering, but Juan was calm.

"Listen, my Captain," Juan said. "If anyone owes this debt to the Republic of Mexico, it is I. Kill me, but let this *pobrecito* go." Corona ignored him and continued with his preparations.

The two men were stood against a rock cliff facing the riflemen of the *'Cordada*. One of these, who had ridden, slept, and eaten with both men, fumbled with his rifle and finally dropped it from his shaking hands. Others showed signs of weakening also, but Corona held them sternly to their task. At the command "Fire!" the crash of rifle shots echoed and re-echoed against the cliffs of the Río Grande like a roll of drums, and there were two smalltime bandits who would ride the dim trails no more.

There is little more to tell. Picho, after seeing three

of his brothers die at the hands of the law, shows signs of reforming. Another brother is working hard in Texas and in 1940 registered for the draft, which just about accounts for the Domínguez family. But there are others with a strain of the old wild Indians in them, and so long as the blood of that stubborn and dissident breed seethes in their veins, we may expect rebels against the existing order, whatever that order may be.

6. *Despedida:* Farewell

Many place names hereabouts are Spanish. You have only to translate them into English and there you are. Many are named for plants, trees, or shrubs. For instance, there are three creeks named respectively Alamo, Tornillo, and Maravillas, all names of trees or plants—the cottonwood, the screw bean, and the marigold. Some places are named for men who are now dead, but who are still remembered by living people. Examples are Pulliam's Bluff, Reed's Trail, and McKinney Creek. Some are named for their appearance, like Mule Ears, Packsaddle, and Elephant Mountain.

It is when you get into those names that have a story or maybe stories connected with them that there is room for controversy. I shall mention three of these briefly. They are Butcher Knife Flat, Dog Canyon, and Smallpox Spring.

One story says Butcher Knife Flat was named back in the '80's when somebody found an old, rusty butcher knife there. Another says it is so named because one Mexican mule skinner killed another on this flat with a butcher knife.

Still another explanation is this: On the northwest edge of this flat there is a sharp-edged mountain, at the foot of which there was a spring, now a well and windmill. Tradition says that in the days of the Apaches and the Mexican traders, this mountain was called *El Cuchillo*, because of its sharp edge. *Cuchillo* translates into English as a butcher or similar knife. So the mountain, the spring, and the broad valley all came to be called Cuchillo or Butcher Knife. At present only the valley is so called.

As for Dog Canyon, one story is of a lost yoke of oxen that was finally found. With the oxen was a stray and apparently lost dog. He seemed to know that if he stayed with these gentle oxen long enough, some human would finally find him. This took place, it is said, on the canyon now known as Dog Canyon. Another story is of a ranchman who once lived on this canyon;

he was a trapper and lion hunter on the side and kept almost as many dogs as he had horses and cattle. He himself was nicknamed "Dog" and the canyon still carries that name.

Smallpox Spring no longer flows, but there are a well and windmill there now. The explanation usually offered is that a whole camp of Mexicans died there of smallpox. But old Mexicans have told me that the spring, creek, and the whole region took its name, as in the case of Butcher Knife, from a nearby mountain. This mountain is of a grayish color, mostly vegetation, but its sides are covered with huge piles of reddish rocks which against the lighter background give the impression of a bad case of smallpox. This mountain, it is said, was called *La Viruela,* which means "smallpox," back in the days of the Apaches. Only the spring seems to have kept its name.

These three examples illustrate the different stories that have grown up around various places in this region. Obviously they cannot all be true.

How these contradictory stories about names, Indians, bandits, and everything else get started is anybody's guess. There are local Munchausens who enjoy telling tall tales to credulous listeners. Very funny at the time! Not so amusing after they are widely published as fact.

Though Baron Munchausen is no longer with us, his

disciples still stalk the earth. And though the bones of that arch liar and braggart be amoldering, his soul goes marching as blithely as any gal drum major, and, like the Wandering Jew, it seems destined to go on to the end of time.

Of course there is always a chance that some one of these yarns is the true one, or at least has a foundation of truth, even though details may be kind of cockeyed. My method is to listen to a story or read it closely, compare it with other stories and with known facts, and then tell it the way I heard it.